TO GO
THINKING SKILLS

Ages 6-8

Activities and ideas to develop thinking skills
across the National Curriculum

Sharon Shapiro

Advisor: Trevor Davies

A & C Black • London

CONTENTS

INTRODUCTION

Today's pupils are the problem solvers of the future. If children are taught factual knowledge only, they tend to respond with conventionally 'correct' answers rather than by exploring creative solutions. All pupils can learn to think critically and creatively. This book provides teachers with straightforward ideas and activities to help pupils develop these skills. The activities make an ideal complement to classroom work across the curriculum. They can be used in isolation, in sequence, or dipped into, as teachers require.

ABOUT THIS BOOK

TEACHERS' FILE

The teachers' file offers advice on how to make make the most of this book. It explains the different types of thinking strategies and how children can benefit from using them. There are ICT tips, assessment ideas and suggestions for parental involvement.

QUICK STARTS

This section offers activity and game ideas that help to promote children's thinking skills. These activities require little or no preparation and can be used across various learning areas to complement existing lesson plans.

ACTIVITY BANK

The activity bank contains 29 photocopiable activities that cover thinking skills related to fluency, flexibility, categorising, questioning, imaginative visualisation, creative thinking, originality and connecting unrelated objects. The activities can be used in any order and can be used by children working individually or in groups.

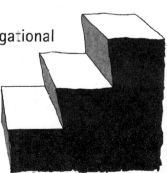
Photocopiable activities

CHALLENGES

These photocopiable task cards offer creative investigational challenges. They can be given to individual pupils or groups, and they can be used at any time and in any order. The task cards are suitable for Key Stage 2 pupils and more able pupils in Key Stage 1, as they require pupils to follow instructions and complete a task independently.

HOW TO USE THIS BOOK

QUICK STARTS

Quick starts are ideal warm-up activities for the beginning of a lesson, similar in principle to the starter activities at the beginning of the daily maths lesson. The activities are designed to be used flexibly: they can be used in any order and at any time, for example, during circle time. Each activity is intended to provide 10–15 minutes of group or whole class discussion.

Example

It won't happen! (page 11) is an ideal small group activity. Afterwards, each group can report back to the whole class. Discuss how many original answers each group thought of.

It won't happen!

Ask pupils to name:
• 10 things they can't hear
• 5 people they will never meet
• 7 things that can't be photographed

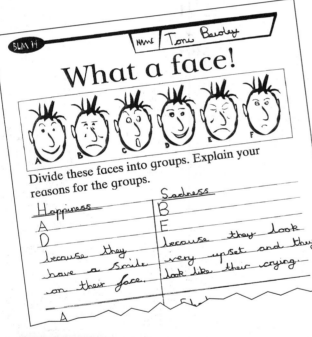

BLM 14   NAME Toni Bewley

What a face!

A B C D E F

Divide these faces into groups. Explain your reasons for the groups.

Happiness	Sadness
A	B
D	E
because they have a smile on their face.	because they look very upset and they look like their crying.
A	

ACTIVITY BANK

These photocopiable activities can be used by individuals, groups or the whole class (with each child or pair of children referring to a copy of the sheet). An activity could provide the focus for a whole lesson; most of the activities require 30–40 minutes' investigation.

Example

What a face! (page 29) offers a number of possible criteria for groupings, the most obvious of which is based on mood. Ask the children to think about what other criteria could be used. Extend the discussion to cover the importance of mood when the children are forming impressions of other people.

CHALLENGES

These activities are perfect for use in learning centres, in the school library or in the classroom. The investigational nature of the activities is in line with National Curriculum requirements such as AT1 in Maths and Science, and supports the development of investigational problem-solving skills.

Example

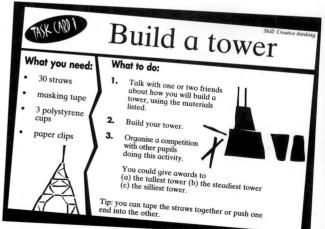

TASK CARD 1   Skill: Creative thinking

Build a tower

What you need:
• 30 straws
• masking tape
• 3 polystyrene cups
• paper clips

What to do:
1. Talk with one or two friends about how you will build a tower, using the materials listed.
2. Build your tower.
3. Organise a competition with other pupils doing this activity.

You could give awards to (a) the tallest tower (b) the steadiest tower (c) the silliest tower.

Tip: you can tape the straws together or push one end into the other.

Build a tower (page 46) is a Design and Technology challenge that is best done as a group activity. Encourage the children to discuss different forms of towers and which type of construction is the most effective.

TEACHERS' FILE

What are thinking skills?

As well as helping children to think clearly, thinking skills enable them to collect information critically and creatively and to use this information to solve problems. Pupils also become more aware of decision-making processes as they develop their thinking skills. Through the activities in this book, children will learn thinking skills that encourage them to look at a variety of ideas, investigate in greater depth, practise more critical decision-making, challenge accepted ideas, approach tasks in decisive ways and search for misunderstandings, while keeping the aims of the task clearly in mind. As a result, their decisions will be more reliable, they will have a deeper understanding of concepts, their ideas will be more creative, they will examine content more critically and their work will be more carefully crafted.

Why do children need to develop thinking skills?

Children need to be able to judge, analyse and think critically in order to participate fully in a democratic and technological society. This can be achieved if the school as a whole recognises the value of thinking skills and provides opportunities for the thinking processes to be modelled and developed. All pupils can improve their thinking abilities, regardless of age, race, socio-economic status or different learning modes.

The basic skills are generally regarded as literacy and numeracy. These involve processes such as computation, recall of facts and the basic mechanics of writing. Once these fundamental skills have been mastered, children need to move on to more challenging tasks that will help them to understand more complex ideas. It is not necessarily true that pupils who can find the correct answers to problems have learned thinking skills. Pupils need plenty of practice before they can tackle problems that require them to use advanced thinking skills. The cognitive operations that make up thinking need to be explored, explained, taught and practised many times before they can be mastered.

Some basic tips

Allow students to be nonconforming and encourage them to complete tasks in their own way. Encourage them to take risks, challenge ideas and to reflect on tasks. If a child learns hundreds of facts but hasn't developed the ability to explore possibilities, much of the knowledge they gain will be wasted.

Thinking 'domains'

Thinking skills can be divided into different areas, or thinking 'domains'. Children need experience of a variety of domains, because each domain has separate aims and develops particular skills. This book offers practice in the following key domains:
- **Critical thinking** encourages children to examine, clarify and evaluate an idea, belief or action. Pupils learn to infer, generalise, take a point of view, hypothesise and find temporary solutions.
- **Decision-making and problem-solving** involve processes such as brainstorming, linking ideas, using analogies, creating original ideas, organising information and looking at a problem from different perspectives. These techniques will enable children to find a variety of solutions to a problem.
- The ability to **collect, retain, recall and use information** when needed is another vital skill.
- **Creative thinking** encourages children to come up with original ideas.

Thinking processes

The activities in this book cover eight processes that are important in promoting thinking skills. These processes can be grouped into cognitive (thinking) and affective (feeling) abilities.

Cognitive abilities
- **Fluency** - thinking of as many ideas as possible
- **Flexibility** - looking at problems from different perspectives; thinking of ways to combine ideas into a new and different solution; grouping objects according to different criteria
- **Originality** - producing unusual or unique ideas
- **Elaboration** - adding or further developing ideas

Affective abilities
- **Curiosity** - working out an idea by instinctively following a certain route
- **Complexity** - thinking of more complex ways of approaching a task, by searching for links, looking for missing sections or restructuring ideas
- **Risk-taking** - making guesses; defending ideas without fear of what others may think
- **Imagining** - picturing and describing something that has never occurred; imagining oneself in other times and places

ASSESSMENT

Allow time for the children to complete activities and give them opportunities to share their ideas in a group. One way in which pupils learn is by mirroring the behaviour and responses of others.
The following are general guidelines for assessing work:
- Display good pieces of work rather than grading them
- Avoid criticising pupils' responses or drawings
- Find something to value whenever possible

Try to achieve continuity in the way pupils are assessed so that information on each child is cumulative and accurate. A progressive file for each child can include details of their strengths, weaknesses and any special achievements. Note carefully any changes, progress or unusual results, especially in highly creative areas such as story-writing, art, special projects, research, inventions or music. Encourage pupils to examine and assess their own abilities and goals, to gain insight into themselves and the way they tackle problems. You could award fun certificates for proficiency in thinking skills (see page 44).

The classroom environment

The classroom environment can be arranged to allow children to express themselves creatively in tasks, exploration and play. It is helpful to organise materials systematically so that pupils have easy access to them. Use open shelving, plastic boxes and cartons for storing activities and resources. Flexible working and seating areas offer children freedom to move around to different areas of the classroom according to the tasks they are completing. If possible, provide separate areas for independent work, small group work and for the whole class to meet. Try changing the shape of these areas to create interest. You could encourage the children to solve problems using shapes such as hexagons, pentagons, spheres and domes in activities that involve making patterns or building towers.

Colours can be used to set the mood for the type of work pupils will be doing in a particular area of the classroom. Red stimulates thought and orange has an energising effect, while yellow should vitalise the children and speed up mental activity. Green and blue are soothing colours that may calm over-excited children. These colours are ideal to incorporate in a quiet reading area.

Thinking skills learning centres

A thinking skills learning centre could be set up in part of the classroom or as a shared resource for the whole school, perhaps in part of the school library. The learning centre might contain games, puzzles, relevant books and a computer with programs for developing thinking skills. It is a good idea to set up folders of blank worksheets and add new ones regularly. Building materials such as Lego® could be available for constructing unusual objects and devices. You could also provide a book in which pupils can record discoveries or useful tips for pupils working there in future.

Ways to enhance the learning environment

Improve the classroom layout and use displays as visual stimuli.
- Select teaching methods and organisational strategies appropriate to the pupils' needs
- Create a learning environment of high challenge and low stress
- Establish a positive, welcoming atmosphere
- Vary the way pupils work – for example, independently or in small groups
- Aim for a balance between structured and unstructured tasks
- Use a variety of learning styles – for example, hands on, visual, oral, written
- Establish the 'big picture' by linking tasks with pupils' experiences
- Use music to enhance the learning environment and to improve the children's ability to recall information

ICT TIPS

Pupils can be motivated by computer games that allow them to show commitment to a task. Simulation or strategy software encourages children to approach tasks open-mindedly and involves players in critical thinking, risk-taking and real life problem-solving.

ICT skills can be integrated into many aspects of learning. ICT is useful for developing problem-solving skills and the associated thinking skills through the use of existing educational software. Spreadsheets and databases can help children to learn more advanced skills while developing lateral thinking and spatial orientation.

Computer versions of board games can also be used to develop thinking skills. Games such as chess and Scrabble® require children to learn rules and use a variety of strategies.

PARENT INVOLVEMENT

It is beneficial to inform parents that their children are learning thinking skills, as well as encouraging them to support their children's learning at home. Explain that thinking skills enable children to deal with complex situations using a range of thinking strategies, and will equip them to continue learning throughout their lives. On a practical level, parents' help can be enlisted in gathering unusual games and puzzles for a thinking skills learning centre (see page 8).

Parents can help their children to develop thinking skills in many ways, for example: providing opportunities to solve problems creatively; involving the children in planning family outings that take into consideration the needs of all family members; and allowing children to participate in family projects such as redesigning rooms. Most importantly, parents can encourage children to be individuals simply by listening to their ideas. Even if the ideas are unusual or impractical, parents can reassure children that their input is valuable. Children will benefit from being part of a family environment where t is acceptable to make mistakes, and where the emphasis is on learning from those mistakes.

QUICK STARTS

Brainstorm!

Have pupils in groups brainstorm the following topics:
- all the things that move
- things that are found underground
- everything that is pink

Emphasise that there are no right or wrong answers and the aim is quantity not quality. Have groups share their answers with the class so that pupils can learn from those who think more divergently.

How could you...?

Have pupils in groups, or as a class, list:
- all the different ways they could travel to school tomorrow
- how they could make people laugh
- other ways to use a magazine besides reading it
- the different uses for a spoonful of peanut butter

Car parts

Using an old but large toy car, ask pupils to imagine it is a full-sized car, and explain that the car no longer works but is being broken into parts. What uses can they think of for the different parts of the car? For example, a front bench seat could become a sofa, tyres could be used as swings, a headlight could become a bedlamp ...

It won't happen!

Ask pupils to name:
- 10 things they can't hear
- 5 people they will never meet
- 7 things that can't be photographed

What's the connection?

Ask pupils to tell you the connection between two line drawings, for example, a picture of rain and a square. In this instance, the square might be a farmer's field that the rain falls on. There is no wrong answer if a link can be explained.

Clever categories

Ask pupils to divide these words into groups, according to categories they decide on:

girl   butter   castle   apple   forest
cake   chair   unicorn   cat   fairy
train   frog   sock   egg   tree   waterfall
bicycle   fire engine

(The words can be written on to a sheet of paper that is photocopied and cut up so each group has a set. This allows pupils to physically move the words between categories and see the effect.)

What if?

Encourage pupils to explore alternatives:

- What if pupils all grew one metre taller in the night?
- What if it rained milk?
- What if people were born old and got younger?

Crazy combinations

Ask pupils to brainstorm a list of different fruit and follow this with a list of different animals. Have pupils work in pairs and ask them to draw an 'anifruit' by combining features of one of the animals and one of the fruits. Have them give their anifruit a name, for example, a combination of an apricot and a cat could be an apricat, or they can just invent a name that feels appropriate.

How do you do it when you haven't got it?

Ask pupils for ideas of how they could:
- brush their hair without a hairbrush or comb
- write a story without pencil or paper
- get dressed without using clothes

Predicting the future

Ask students:
- what they think children will wear to school in 100 years' time
- what they think they will be doing, and where they will be, in 20 years
- how they will travel to school in the future

Imagine that!

- Have pupils cut pictures out of magazines and join different heads, bodies and other items to invent strange people and things.
- Ask pupils to imagine what is inside a house they see in a picture

The inventors

Have pupils invent:

- a new way to brush their hair
- a machine for cleaning a budgie's cage
- a device that wakes them up in the morning and feeds them breakfast

Fix it!

Using an item children are familiar with, for example, a cup or a pencil, ask them to tell you what are its disadvantages (for example, the cup can spill stuff on your face if you tip it up quickly). Have pupils suggest ideas for fixing the problem, for example, a guard that extends from the rim of the cup but leaves room for your mouth. Encourage 'silly' and unusual ideas.

Recycle

Ask pupils what they could do with:

- felt-tip pens that don't write anymore
- a trampoline that has lost its bounce
- cereal that has gone stale

It doesn't matter how silly the ideas are. Encourage pupils to think of as many as they can.

What is the same?

Think of two things that are widely different and ask pupils what these two things have in common, for example a train and an apple. Both can be red; both can be shiny; it's healthy for your body to eat apples, and healthy for the environment to catch a train rather than driving a car . . .

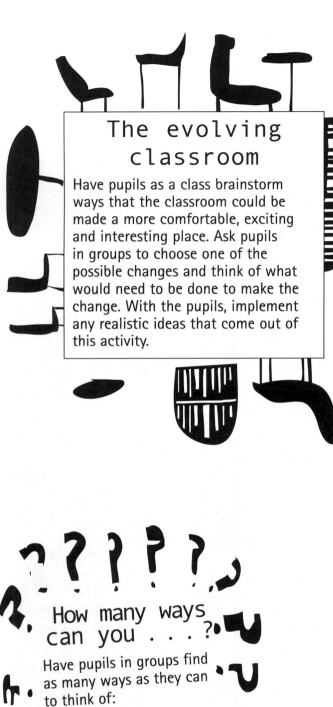

The evolving classroom

Have pupils as a class brainstorm ways that the classroom could be made a more comfortable, exciting and interesting place. Ask pupils in groups to choose one of the possible changes and think of what would need to be done to make the change. With the pupils, implement any realistic ideas that come out of this activity.

BAR

B stands for Bigger/smaller
A stands for Add on
R stands for Replace/rearrange/ change.

For example, draw a shoe. Ask what could be made bigger or smaller, for example, the sole of the shoe could be a platform a metre high, so that they can see over people's heads in a crowd. Add could be wings or a motor, to get them places. R could be the replacement of laces with velcro strips to make it easier to get the shoes off.

Ask pupils to use the BAR process using their bed or a pencil as the object, giving reasons for each change. Encourage silly and innovative ideas.

How many ways can you . . . ?

Have pupils in groups find as many ways as they can to think of:

• getting from their bedroom to the kitchen
• blowing up a balloon
• putting their clothes on.

Reflecting on the day

At the end of each day ask children what they learned during the day, what new things they found out, what they did well, what they could learn to do better. Reinforce the positive aspects of the day. Help children think of something to tell parents about, or ways to use their new thinking skills at home.

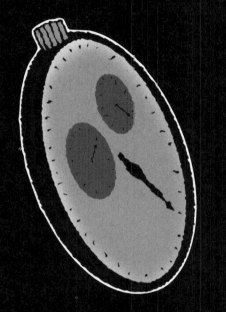

ACTIVITY BANK

Alphabet animals

Find names of animals for each letter of the alphabet. Write as many as you can think of for each letter. For D you could have dog, duck, dinosaur, deer . . .

A _____   N _____

B _____   O _____

C _____   P _____

D _____   Q _____

E _____   R _____

F _____   S _____

G _____   T _____

H _____   U _____

I _____   V _____

J _____   W _____

K _____   X _____

L _____   Y _____

M _____   Z _____

Thinking skill: Fluency

What could it be?

Work in a group to think of all the answers that you can to the questions. See if other children's answers give you more ideas. One child could write a list or tape the answers.

How many things are smaller than your hand? List them.

_____

_____

_____

_____

What can be hidden under your shoe?

_____

_____

_____

What can you balance on your hand?

_____

_____

_____

Thinking skill: Fluency

NAME

What did you see today?

What did you see when you first woke up today? When you walked through the house? On your way to school? List everything you have seen today.

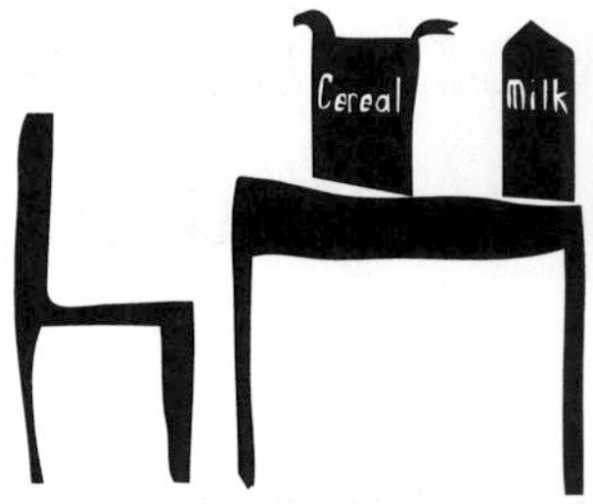

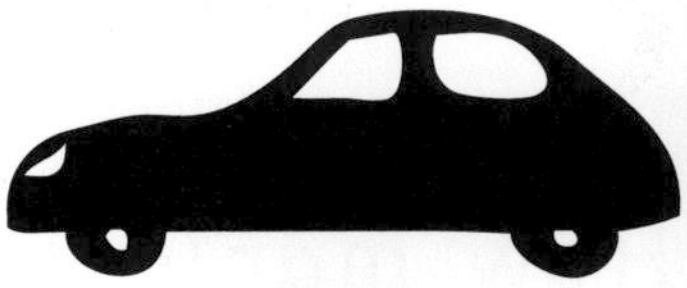

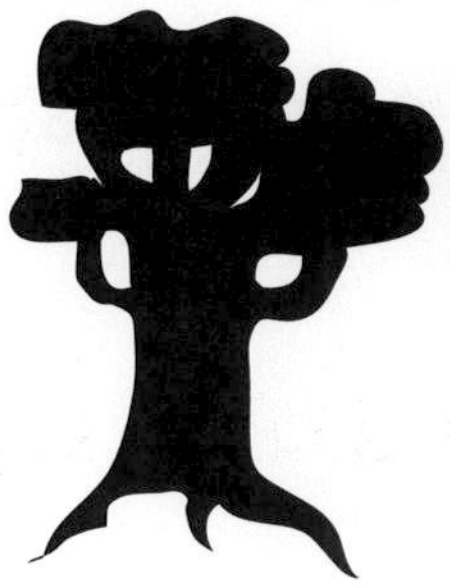

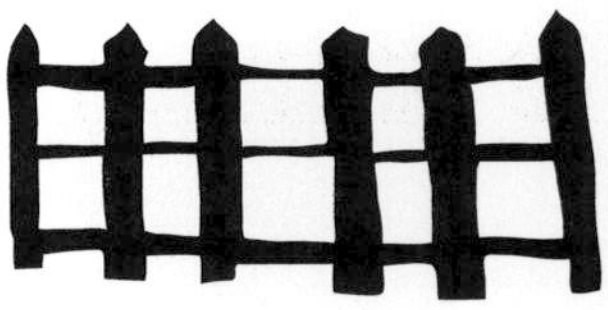

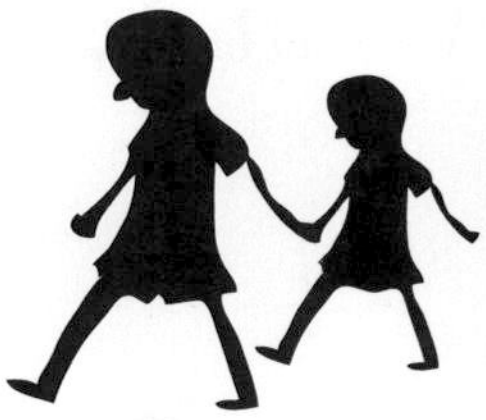

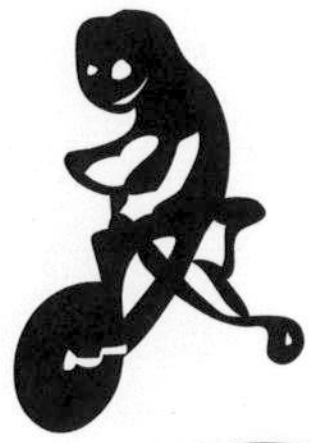

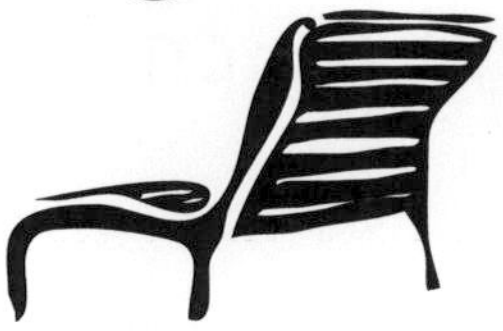

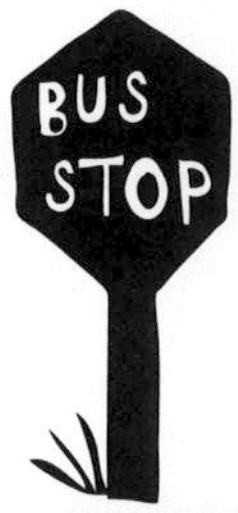

Thinking skill: Fluency

How can you use it?

Work in a small group. Take a paper clip each
and hold it, feel it, open it, bend it, reshape it.

How many different uses can you think of for a paperclip?

hair clip

letter of the alphabet

Thinking skill: Fluency

Do you want a ride?

How many different things can you ride?

_____

_____

_____

_____

_____

_____

List all the things that you can push.

_____

_____

_____

_____

_____

Thinking skill: Fluency

Playing games

Imagine an old tyre. What does it look like? How heavy is it? How does it feel? How does it smell?

How many games can you make up using an old car tyre?

_____

_____

_____

_____

_____

If the tyre was chopped into pieces, what could you use the different bits for? Note that some bits of the tyre are rough, some are smooth and some have letters on them.

_____

_____

_____

_____

_____

Thinking skill: Fluency

Make a picture

Choose a shape and change it into:

a car	a house	an imaginary friend	a dog

Thinking skill: Flexibility

What are these? →

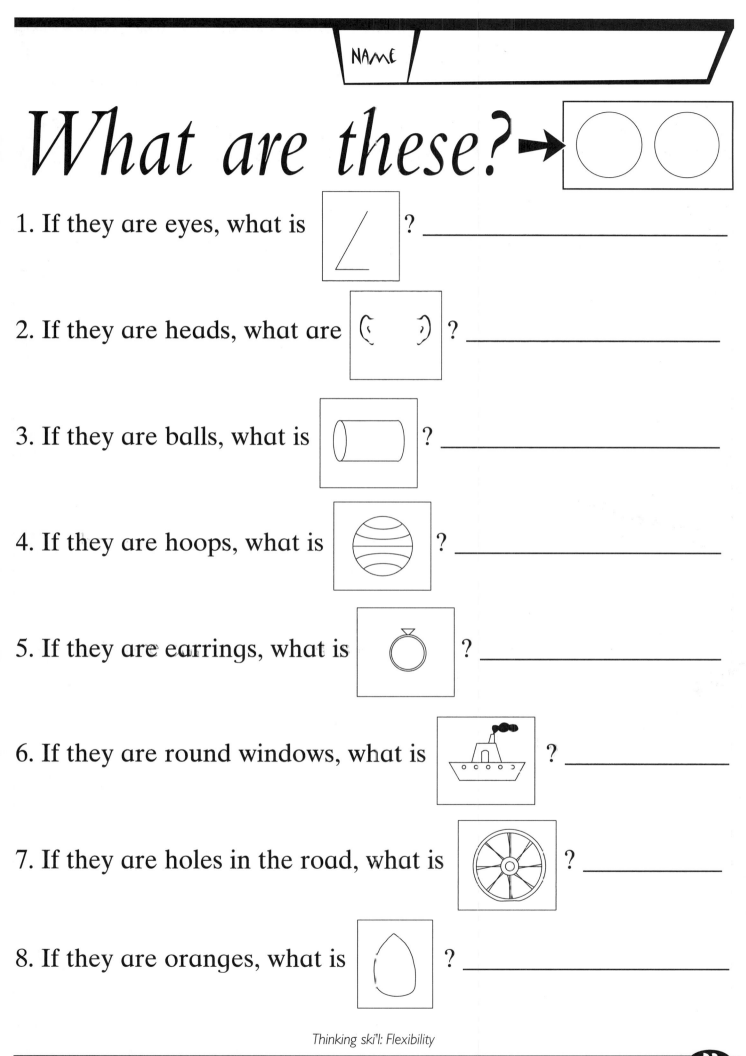

1. If they are eyes, what is [_____] ? _____

2. If they are heads, what are [_____] ? _____

3. If they are balls, what is [_____] ? _____

4. If they are hoops, what is [_____] ? _____

5. If they are earrings, what is [_____] ? _____

6. If they are round windows, what is [_____] ? _____

7. If they are holes in the road, what is [_____] ? _____

8. If they are oranges, what is [_____] ? _____

Thinking skill: Flexibility

A piece of string

Get a 30 cm piece of string from your teacher. Write down all the things you could do with your piece of string.

_____

_____

_____

_____

_____

_____

_____

_____

_____

_____

_____

Thinking skill: Flexibility

The old fire engine

This fire engine is too old to be used as a fire engine anymore. It's going to be pulled to pieces. What could all the pieces be used for?

wheels _____

ladder _____

headlights _____

seats _____

steering wheel _____

windscreen _____

hose _____

other bits _____

Thinking skill: Flexibility

What is the same?
What is different?

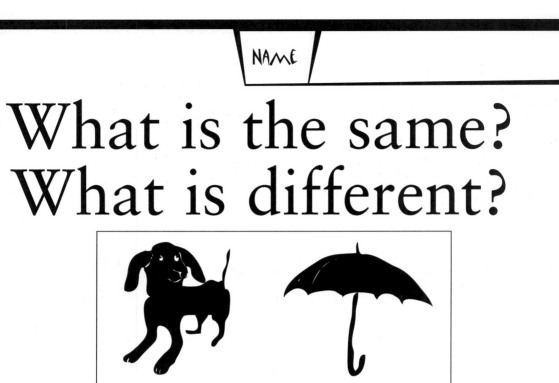

Use the acronym SCUMPS to compare the objects.
List everything that is the same or different.

S = Size _____

_____

C = Colour _____

_____

U = Use _____

_____

M = Materials _____

_____

P = Parts _____

_____

S = Shape _____

_____

Thinking skill: Flexibility

The pink shirt

Your grandmother has given you a pink shirt for your birthday. You hate it. You don't want to hurt her feelings but you don't want to wear it.

Write five good excuses why you can't wear the shirt.

_____

_____

_____

_____

_____

_____

_____

Write five ways you could use the shirt instead of wearing it.

_____

_____

_____

_____

_____

_____

_____

Thinking skiil: Flexibility

What can it be used for?

Write at least ten uses for a tennis ball.
They can be as silly as you like.

Thinking skill: Flexibility

What a face!

Divide these faces into groups. Explain your reasons for the groups.

_____

_____

_____

_____

_____

_____

_____

_____

_____

_____

_____

_____

Thinking skill: Categorising

You ask the questions

The answer is 'A rose'. Write at least three questions.

The answer is 'In the middle of the night'.
Write at least three questions.

Thinking skill: Questioning

What can it be?

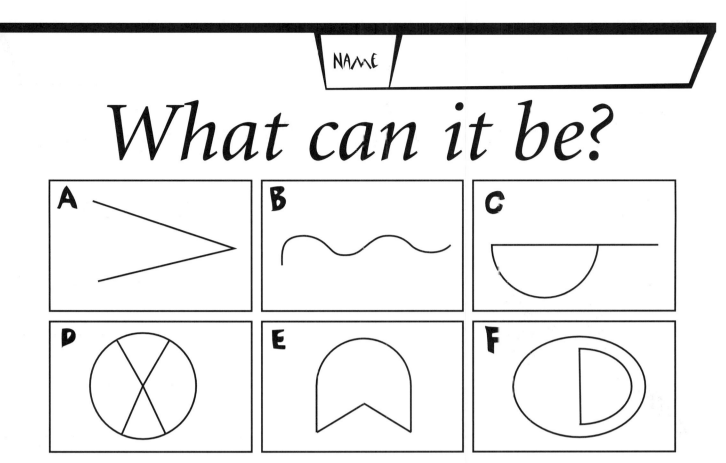

Look at the pictures and write what you think they could be. You can look at them upside-down or any other way.

It's something to do with school. What is it?	It's something to do with the holidays. What is it?
A _____	A _____
B _____	B _____
C _____	C _____
D _____	D _____
E _____	E _____
F _____	F _____

Thinking skill: Imaginative visualisation

The trancapar

Draw a trancapar. (There is no such thing as a trancapar so it can be anything you like.)

Tell the story of what happened to the trancapar last Tuesday.

_____

_____

_____

_____

_____

Thinking skill: Imaginative visualisation

What are these splodges?

'This is a baby bird with its beak open. It is crying for food.'

Write in the space what each splodge could be.

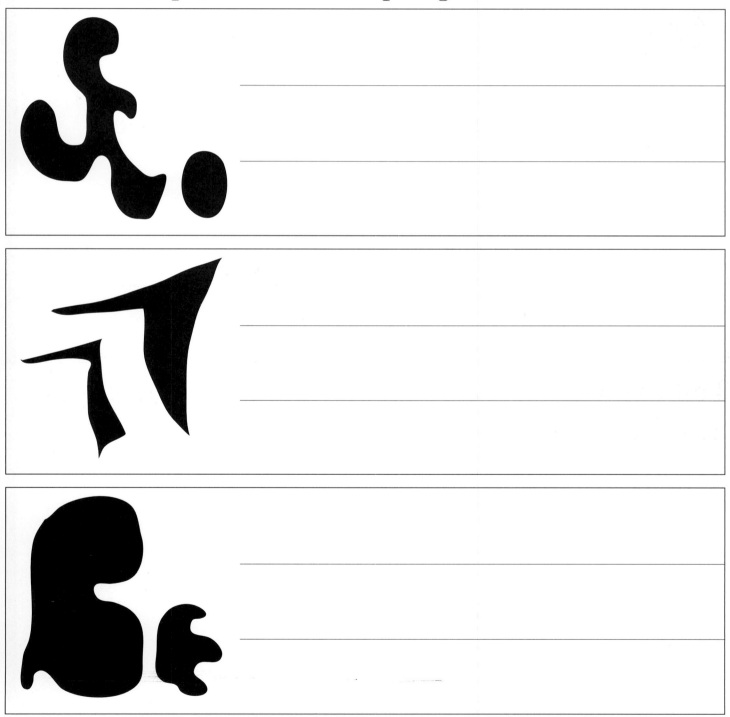

Thinking skill: Imaginative visualisation

Create a picture

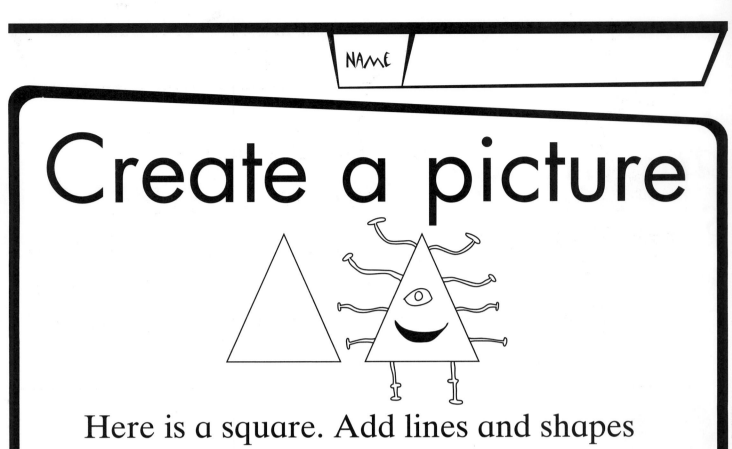

Here is a square. Add lines and shapes to make a picture.

Thinking skill: Imaginative visualisation

NAME

Jack and the beanstalk

Imagine that Jack is climbing up the beanstalk. Draw four different pictures of what he might see as he climbs higher and higher.

Thinking skill: Imaginative visualisation

NAME

Is it a ghost?

Write down all the things that this cloud looks like.

_____

_____

_____

_____

_____

_____

_____

_____

Thinking skill: Imaginative visualisation

Change the chair

Redesign the chair using the BAR system.

B = make bigger or smaller

A = add something

R = remove something and replace it with something else

	B
	Reasons _____

A	**R**
Reasons _____	*Reasons* _____

Thinking skill: Creative thinking

NAME

Help the kangaroo

A kangaroo hurt its leg while hopping in the zoo. It can't move and needs to be taken to a vet. Draw four different ways of moving the kangaroo so that it can be taken to the vet. Label each drawing.

Thinking skill: Creative thinking

Toothpick tricks

a hut   a bed   a kite

Try making different pictures. Use no more than six toothpicks for each. (No breaking the toothpicks!) Use glue to stick your favourite picture to the page.

Some you could try: a fan, an insect, a flag, a dog, a spaceship, a fish, a windmill, a tent

Thinking skill: Creative thinking

Blast into space

Make something that can be used in space.

You'll need:

- a box
- 2 cotton reels
- a cup
- glue stick or sticky tape
- a pair of scissors
- other objects available in your classroom

Draw your design for the thing you are going to make in the box below, then build it.

Thinking skill: Creative thinking

What is THAT?

Make up a new and strange animal and draw it here.

What is it called?

Where does it live?

What does it eat?

Thinking skill: Originality

Join the pictures

1. If picture 1 is a finger, what is 4? _____

2. If picture 7 is a mountain, what is 6? _____

3. If picture 2 is a tooth, what is 3? _____

4. If 8 is a kennel, what is 9? _____

5. If 4 is a hat (you are looking down on it), what is 5? _____

_____

6. If 8 is an igloo, what is 4? _____

7. If picture 8 shows two rocks, what is 1? _____

8. If 5 is a door (turn the page sideways), what do you see when you

   open the door at picture 9? _____

Thinking skill: Originality

What a tale!

Make up a story about the toaster and the cat. You can add other things as you go.

_____

_____

_____

_____

_____

_____

_____

_____

_____

Thinking skill: Connecting unrelated objects

Thinking skills awards

Awarded to

_____

Terrific thinking!

Signed _____

Date _____

Awarded to

_____

Good idea!

Signed _____

Date _____

Awarded to

_____

Great imagination!

Signed _____

Date _____

Awarded to

_____

Clever question!

Signed _____

Date _____

CHALLENGES

TASK CARD 1

Build a tower

What you need:

- 30 straws
- masking tape
- 3 polystyrene cups
- paper clips

What to do:

1. Talk with one or two friends about how you will build a tower using the materials listed.

2. Build your tower.

3. Organise a competition with other pupils doing this activity.
   You could give awards to (a) the tallest tower; (b) the steadiest tower; (c) the silliest tower.

Tip: you can tape the straws together or push one end into the other.

TASK CARD 2

Blind drawing

What you need:

- a blindfold
- a large piece of paper
- a pencil

What to do:

1. Put your paper and pencil in front of you on the desk. Decide what you are going to draw, then blindfold your eyes. Make sure you can't see at all.

2. When you have finished, take the blindfold off and look at your drawing. DON'T RUB OUT ANY LINES!

3. Finish the picture by adding extra lines, colour or decorations.

4. Here are some things you could try drawing: a person's face with two eyes, a nose and mouth; a tree, two flowers and the sun; an animal sitting on some grass; the moon, stars and a rocket ship. Think of your own as well!

TASK CARD 3 — Create an animal

What you need:

- a milk carton
- a paper plate
- scissors
- glue

What to do:

1. Decide on the animal you want to make.
2. Find a picture in a book or draw what it will look like.
3. Decide which way the carton will stand. Does the animal have a long or short body? Is it tall? How many legs and eyes does it have? Does it have a tail?
4. Cut the paper plate into the pieces you need. Think of the shape and size of the parts you are making. Is it rough or smooth? Choose the parts of the plate that you need. Do you need to fold as well as cut it?
5. Glue your animal together. When it has dried, paint the body and decorate it.

TASK CARD 4 — Question time

What to do:

1. Choose one person to sit in front (the caller) and one person to keep count of how many questions have been asked (the counter). The rest of the group sit in front of the caller.

2. The caller chooses an animal, thing or famous person but must not tell anyone else what or who it is.

3. The rest of the group ask questions to try to guess what or who it is. They have to be questions that have the answer 'yes' or 'no'. (If the caller doesn't know, it doesn't count as a question.) The group gets 15 questions.

4. If the group can't guess it, the caller says what it was and has another turn. If someone guesses the right answer, the caller sits down and the person with the correct answer takes their place. Change the counter for each game.

TASK CARD 5
The Infobot, part 1

What you need:

- pencil
- paper
- cardboard boxes
- glue
- magazines
- nails
- knobs
- springs
- paper cups
- string
- other scrap materials

What to do:

1. Think about what you want your robot to look like. What body parts might it have? How could you make them using the materials that you have?

2. Draw a picture (a design) of what you want your robot to look like.

3. Build your robot's body and add anything else you wish. You might like to make a sign that says 'Ask the Infobot!'

Bees live in a beehive.

TASK CARD 6
The Infobot, part 2

What you need:
- your robot
- a tape recorder
- a blank tape

What to do:

1. Research a topic that you are interested in, for example, netball, the solar system, dinosaurs. Collect all the interesting information on it that you can. Keep notes on what you find out.

2. Select what information you want to pass on, and put it in an order you think will help others understand it.

3. Record the information clearly on to the blank tape. (Ask your teacher to help you.)

4. Label the tape and place the recorder behind the Infobot. Other students can sit in front of the Infobot and listen to the tape.